THIS *meal* PLANNER BELONGS TO:

____

____

Email us at FREEBIES@JUNELUCY.COM
to get a FREE printable download!

FOR A LITTLE INSPIRATION
follow along at:

@JUNEANDLUCY

@JUNEANDLUCY

WWW.JUNELUCY.COM

Shop our other books at
www.junelucy.com

Wholesale distribution through Ingram Content Group
www.ingramcontent.com/publishers/distribution/wholesale

For questions and customer service, email us at
support@junelucy.com

Kitchen CHEAT SHEET

MEASUREMENT CONVERSIONS

TSP	TBSP	FL OZ	CUP	PINT	QUART	GALLON	ML
3	1	1/2	1/16	1/32	-	-	15
6	2	1	1/8	1/16	1/32	-	30
12	4	2	1/4	1/8	1/16	-	60
18	6	3	3/8	-	-	-	90
24	8	4	1/2	1/4	1/8	1/32	120
36	12	6	3/4	-	-	-	175
48	16	8	1	1/2	1/4	1/16	240
96	32	16	2	1	1/2	1/8	480
-	64	32	4	2	1	1/4	960
-	256	128	16	8	4	1	3840

EMERGENCY SUBSTITUTIONS

INSTEAD OF THIS...	USE THIS...
BAKING POWDER (1 TSP)	1/2 TSP CREAM OF TARTAR PLUS 1/4 TSP BAKING SODA
BUTTERMILK (1 CUP)	1 TBSP LEMON JUICE OR VINEGAR + ENOUGH MILK TO MAKE 1 CUP
CORNSTARCH (1 TBSP)	2 TBSP ALL-PURPOSE FLOUR
EGG (1 WHOLE)	2 EGG WHITES OR 2 EGG YOLKS
SELF-RISING FLOUR (1 CUP)	1 CUP ALL-PURPOSE FLOUR + 1 TSP BAKING POWDER
FRESH GARLIC (1 CLOVE)	1/8 TSP GARLIC POWDER
FRESH HERBS (1 TBSP)	1/2-1 TSP CRUSHED DRIED HERBS
SOUR CREAM (1 CUP)	1 CUP PLAIN YOGURT
LEMON JUICE (1 TSP)	1/2 TSP VINEGAR

WHAT'S COOKING?

	breakfast	lunch	dinner	snacks
MONDAY				
TUESDAY				
WEDNESDAY				
THURSDAY				
FRIDAY				
SATURDAY				
SUNDAY				

groceries

NOTES

WHAT'S COOKING?

	breakfast	lunch	dinner	snacks
MONDAY				
TUESDAY				
WEDNESDAY				
THURSDAY				
FRIDAY				
SATURDAY				
SUNDAY				

groceries

NOTES

WHAT'S COOKING?

	breakfast	lunch	dinner	snacks
MONDAY				
TUESDAY				
WEDNESDAY				
THURSDAY				
FRIDAY				
SATURDAY				
SUNDAY				

groceries

NOTES

WHAT'S COOKING?

	breakfast	lunch	dinner	snacks
MONDAY				
TUESDAY				
WEDNESDAY				
THURSDAY				
FRIDAY				
SATURDAY				
SUNDAY				

groceries

NOTES

WHAT'S COOKING?

	breakfast	lunch	dinner	snacks
MONDAY				
TUESDAY				
WEDNESDAY				
THURSDAY				
FRIDAY				
SATURDAY				
SUNDAY				

groceries

NOTES

WHAT'S COOKING?

	breakfast	lunch	dinner	snacks
MONDAY				
TUESDAY				
WEDNESDAY				
THURSDAY				
FRIDAY				
SATURDAY				
SUNDAY				

groceries

NOTES

WHAT'S COOKING?

	breakfast	lunch	dinner	snacks
MONDAY				
TUESDAY				
WEDNESDAY				
THURSDAY				
FRIDAY				
SATURDAY				
SUNDAY				

groceries

NOTES

WHAT'S COOKING?

	breakfast	lunch	dinner	snacks
MONDAY				
TUESDAY				
WEDNESDAY				
THURSDAY				
FRIDAY				
SATURDAY				
SUNDAY				

groceries

NOTES

WHAT'S COOKING?

	breakfast	lunch	dinner	snacks
MONDAY				
TUESDAY				
WEDNESDAY				
THURSDAY				
FRIDAY				
SATURDAY				
SUNDAY				

groceries

NOTES

WHAT'S COOKING?

	breakfast	lunch	dinner	snacks
MONDAY				
TUESDAY				
WEDNESDAY				
THURSDAY				
FRIDAY				
SATURDAY				
SUNDAY				

groceries

NOTES

WHAT'S COOKING?

	breakfast	lunch	dinner	snacks
MONDAY				
TUESDAY				
WEDNESDAY				
THURSDAY				
FRIDAY				
SATURDAY				
SUNDAY				

groceries

NOTES

WHAT'S COOKING?

	breakfast	lunch	dinner	snacks
MONDAY				
TUESDAY				
WEDNESDAY				
THURSDAY				
FRIDAY				
SATURDAY				
SUNDAY				

groceries

NOTES

WHAT'S COOKING?

	breakfast	lunch	dinner	snacks
MONDAY				
TUESDAY				
WEDNESDAY				
THURSDAY				
FRIDAY				
SATURDAY				
SUNDAY				

groceries

NOTES

WHAT'S COOKING?

	breakfast	lunch	dinner	snacks
MONDAY				
TUESDAY				
WEDNESDAY				
THURSDAY				
FRIDAY				
SATURDAY				
SUNDAY				

groceries

NOTES

WHAT'S COOKING?

	breakfast	lunch	dinner	snacks
MONDAY				
TUESDAY				
WEDNESDAY				
THURSDAY				
FRIDAY				
SATURDAY				
SUNDAY				

groceries

NOTES

WHAT'S COOKING?

	breakfast	lunch	dinner	snacks
MONDAY				
TUESDAY				
WEDNESDAY				
THURSDAY				
FRIDAY				
SATURDAY				
SUNDAY				

groceries

NOTES

WHAT'S COOKING?

	breakfast	lunch	dinner	snacks
MONDAY				
TUESDAY				
WEDNESDAY				
THURSDAY				
FRIDAY				
SATURDAY				
SUNDAY				

groceries

NOTES

WHAT'S COOKING?

	breakfast	lunch	dinner	snacks
MONDAY				
TUESDAY				
WEDNESDAY				
THURSDAY				
FRIDAY				
SATURDAY				
SUNDAY				

groceries

NOTES

WHAT'S COOKING?

	breakfast	lunch	dinner	snacks
MONDAY				
TUESDAY				
WEDNESDAY				
THURSDAY				
FRIDAY				
SATURDAY				
SUNDAY				

groceries

NOTES

WHAT'S COOKING?

	breakfast	lunch	dinner	snacks
MONDAY				
TUESDAY				
WEDNESDAY				
THURSDAY				
FRIDAY				
SATURDAY				
SUNDAY				

groceries

NOTES

WHAT'S COOKING?

	breakfast	lunch	dinner	snacks
MONDAY				
TUESDAY				
WEDNESDAY				
THURSDAY				
FRIDAY				
SATURDAY				
SUNDAY				

groceries

NOTES

WHAT'S COOKING?

	breakfast	lunch	dinner	snacks
MONDAY				
TUESDAY				
WEDNESDAY				
THURSDAY				
FRIDAY				
SATURDAY				
SUNDAY				

groceries

NOTES

WHAT'S COOKING?

	breakfast	lunch	dinner	snacks
MONDAY				
TUESDAY				
WEDNESDAY				
THURSDAY				
FRIDAY				
SATURDAY				
SUNDAY				

groceries

NOTES

WHAT'S COOKING?

	breakfast	lunch	dinner	snacks
MONDAY				
TUESDAY				
WEDNESDAY				
THURSDAY				
FRIDAY				
SATURDAY				
SUNDAY				

groceries

NOTES

WHAT'S COOKING?

	breakfast	lunch	dinner	snacks
MONDAY				
TUESDAY				
WEDNESDAY				
THURSDAY				
FRIDAY				
SATURDAY				
SUNDAY				

groceries

NOTES

WHAT'S COOKING?

	breakfast	lunch	dinner	snacks
MONDAY				
TUESDAY				
WEDNESDAY				
THURSDAY				
FRIDAY				
SATURDAY				
SUNDAY				

groceries

NOTES

WHAT'S COOKING?

	breakfast	lunch	dinner	snacks
MONDAY				
TUESDAY				
WEDNESDAY				
THURSDAY				
FRIDAY				
SATURDAY				
SUNDAY				

groceries

NOTES

WHAT'S COOKING?

	breakfast	lunch	dinner	snacks
MONDAY				
TUESDAY				
WEDNESDAY				
THURSDAY				
FRIDAY				
SATURDAY				
SUNDAY				

groceries

NOTES

WHAT'S COOKING?

	breakfast	lunch	dinner	snacks
MONDAY				
TUESDAY				
WEDNESDAY				
THURSDAY				
FRIDAY				
SATURDAY				
SUNDAY				

Groceries

NOTES

WHAT'S COOKING?

	breakfast	lunch	dinner	snacks
MONDAY				
TUESDAY				
WEDNESDAY				
THURSDAY				
FRIDAY				
SATURDAY				
SUNDAY				

groceries

NOTES

WHAT'S COOKING?

	breakfast	lunch	dinner	snacks
MONDAY				
TUESDAY				
WEDNESDAY				
THURSDAY				
FRIDAY				
SATURDAY				
SUNDAY				

groceries

NOTES

WHAT'S COOKING?

	breakfast	lunch	dinner	snacks
MONDAY				
TUESDAY				
WEDNESDAY				
THURSDAY				
FRIDAY				
SATURDAY				
SUNDAY				

groceries

NOTES

WHAT'S COOKING?

	breakfast	lunch	dinner	snacks
MONDAY				
TUESDAY				
WEDNESDAY				
THURSDAY				
FRIDAY				
SATURDAY				
SUNDAY				

groceries

NOTES

WHAT'S COOKING?

	breakfast	lunch	dinner	snacks
MONDAY				
TUESDAY				
WEDNESDAY				
THURSDAY				
FRIDAY				
SATURDAY				
SUNDAY				

groceries

- [ ]
- [ ]
- [ ]
- [ ]
- [ ]
- [ ]
- [ ]
- [ ]
- [ ]
- [ ]
- [ ]
- [ ]
- [ ]
- [ ]
- [ ]
- [ ]
- [ ]
- [ ]
- [ ]
- [ ]

NOTES

WHAT'S COOKING?

	breakfast	lunch	dinner	snacks
MONDAY				
TUESDAY				
WEDNESDAY				
THURSDAY				
FRIDAY				
SATURDAY				
SUNDAY				

groceries

NOTES

WHAT'S COOKING?

	breakfast	lunch	dinner	snacks
MONDAY				
TUESDAY				
WEDNESDAY				
THURSDAY				
FRIDAY				
SATURDAY				
SUNDAY				

groceries

NOTES

WHAT'S COOKING?

	breakfast	lunch	dinner	snacks
MONDAY				
TUESDAY				
WEDNESDAY				
THURSDAY				
FRIDAY				
SATURDAY				
SUNDAY				

groceries

NOTES

WHAT'S COOKING?

	breakfast	lunch	dinner	snacks
MONDAY				
TUESDAY				
WEDNESDAY				
THURSDAY				
FRIDAY				
SATURDAY				
SUNDAY				

groceries

NOTES

WHAT'S COOKING?

	breakfast	lunch	dinner	snacks
MONDAY				
TUESDAY				
WEDNESDAY				
THURSDAY				
FRIDAY				
SATURDAY				
SUNDAY				

groceries

NOTES

WHAT'S COOKING?

	breakfast	lunch	dinner	snacks
MONDAY				
TUESDAY				
WEDNESDAY				
THURSDAY				
FRIDAY				
SATURDAY				
SUNDAY				

groceries

NOTES

WHAT'S COOKING?

	breakfast	lunch	dinner	snacks
MONDAY				
TUESDAY				
WEDNESDAY				
THURSDAY				
FRIDAY				
SATURDAY				
SUNDAY				

groceries

NOTES

WHAT'S COOKING?

	breakfast	lunch	dinner	snacks
MONDAY				
TUESDAY				
WEDNESDAY				
THURSDAY				
FRIDAY				
SATURDAY				
SUNDAY				

groceries

NOTES

WHAT'S COOKING?

	breakfast	lunch	dinner	snacks
MONDAY				
TUESDAY				
WEDNESDAY				
THURSDAY				
FRIDAY				
SATURDAY				
SUNDAY				

groceries

NOTES

WHAT'S COOKING?

	breakfast	lunch	dinner	snacks
MONDAY				
TUESDAY				
WEDNESDAY				
THURSDAY				
FRIDAY				
SATURDAY				
SUNDAY				

groceries

NOTES

WHAT'S COOKING?

	breakfast	lunch	dinner	snacks
MONDAY				
TUESDAY				
WEDNESDAY				
THURSDAY				
FRIDAY				
SATURDAY				
SUNDAY				

groceries

NOTES

WHAT'S COOKING?

	breakfast	lunch	dinner	snacks
MONDAY				
TUESDAY				
WEDNESDAY				
THURSDAY				
FRIDAY				
SATURDAY				
SUNDAY				

groceries

NOTES

WHAT'S COOKING?

	breakfast	lunch	dinner	snacks
MONDAY				
TUESDAY				
WEDNESDAY				
THURSDAY				
FRIDAY				
SATURDAY				
SUNDAY				

groceries

NOTES

WHAT'S COOKING?

	breakfast	lunch	dinner	snacks
MONDAY				
TUESDAY				
WEDNESDAY				
THURSDAY				
FRIDAY				
SATURDAY				
SUNDAY				

groceries

NOTES

WHAT'S COOKING?

	breakfast	lunch	dinner	snacks
MONDAY				
TUESDAY				
WEDNESDAY				
THURSDAY				
FRIDAY				
SATURDAY				
SUNDAY				

groceries

NOTES

WHAT'S COOKING?

	breakfast	lunch	dinner	snacks
MONDAY				
TUESDAY				
WEDNESDAY				
THURSDAY				
FRIDAY				
SATURDAY				
SUNDAY				

groceries

- ○ ____
- ○ ____
- ○ ____
- ○ ____
- ○ ____
- ○ ____
- ○ ____
- ○ ____
- ○ ____
- ○ ____
- ○ ____
- ○ ____
- ○ ____
- ○ ____
- ○ ____
- ○ ____
- ○ ____
- ○ ____
- ○ ____
- ○ ____
- ○ ____
- ○ ____
- ○ ____
- ○ ____
- ○ ____
- ○ ____
- ○ ____
- ○ ____
- ○ ____
- ○ ____
- ○ ____
- ○ ____
- ○ ____
- ○ ____
- ○ ____
- ○ ____
- ○ ____
- ○ ____
- ○ ____
- ○ ____

NOTES

WHAT'S COOKING?

	breakfast	lunch	dinner	snacks
MONDAY				
TUESDAY				
WEDNESDAY				
THURSDAY				
FRIDAY				
SATURDAY				
SUNDAY				

groceries

NOTES

WHAT'S COOKING?

	breakfast	lunch	dinner	snacks
MONDAY				
TUESDAY				
WEDNESDAY				
THURSDAY				
FRIDAY				
SATURDAY				
SUNDAY				

groceries

NOTES

Made in the USA
San Bernardino, CA
06 August 2020

76581154R10062